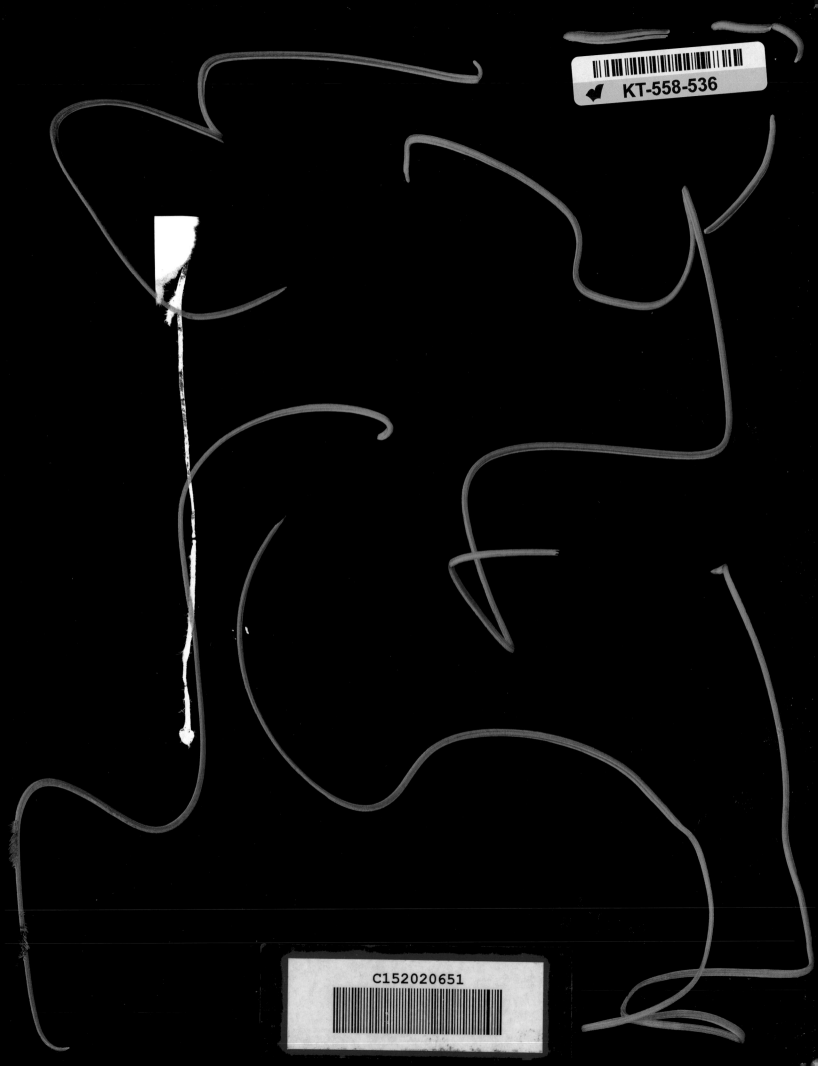

20TH CENTURY
fashion
THE '70S

PUNKS, GLAM ROCKERS
& NEW ROMANTICS

20TH CENTURY FASHION – THE '70s
was produced by

David West ㋛ **Children's Books**
7 Princeton Court
55 Felsham Road
London SW15 1AZ

Picture Research: Carlotta Cooper, Brooks Krikler
Research
Editor: Clare Oliver
Consultant: Helen Reynolds

First published in Great Britain in 1999 by
Heinemann Library, Halley Court, Jordan Hill,
Oxford OX2 8EJ, a division of Reed Educational and
Professional Publishing Limited.

OXFORD MELBOURNE AUCKLAND
JOHANNESBURG BLANTYRE GABORONE
IBADAN PORTSMOUTH (NH) USA CHICAGO

03 02 01
10 9 8 7 6 5 4 3

ISBN 0 431 09552 3 (HB)
ISBN 0 431 09559 0 (PB)

British Library Cataloguing in Publication Data

Gilmour, Sarah
Punks, glam rockers and new romantics (1970s). -
(Fashion in the twentieth century)
1. Fashion - History - 20th century - Juvenile
literature
2. Costume - 20th century - Juvenile literature
I. Title
391'.009047

Printed and bound in Italy.

PHOTO CREDITS :
Abbreviations: t-top, m-middle,
b-bottom, r-right, l-left
Covertl & pages: 3tl, 14r ,15mr,
16-17 : Frank Spooner Pictures;
cover ml & pages 3ml, 4-5, 10tl,
11br, 16tl, 18bl, 20r, 20-21, 22bl
& r, 23l, 24bl, 24-25, 25br:
Redferns; Cover bl.1, 16bl, 17mr:
Albert Watson © Vogue/Condé
Nast Publications Ltd; Cover bl.2,
8bl, 11tr, 13br: Barry Lategan ©
Vogue/Condé Nast Publications
Ltd; Cover bm, 8br, 26tl, 26-27,
27tr: Clive Arrowsmith ©
Vogue/Condé Nast Publications
Ltd; Cover br, 3mr, 9m, 18r, 23mr,
29bl: Lothar Schmid ©
Vogue/Condé Nast Publications
Ltd; Cover br, 15br, 25tr, 26bl:
Willie Christie © Vogue/Condé
Nast Publications Ltd; 4br, 5tr,
5br, 5bl, 10-11, 12bl, 12-13, 19br,
20bl, 21tl, 22tl, 28bl, 28br:
Hulton Getty; 6tl: Sarah Moon ©
Vogue/Condé Nast Publications
Ltd; 6br: Henry Clarke ©
Vogue/Condé Nast Publications
Ltd; 6-7: Jonvelle © Vogue/Condé
Nast Publications Ltd; 7br, 28tl,
29rm: Arthur Elgort ©
Vogue/Condé Nast Publications
Ltd; 7tr, 13tl, 19tr: Kobal
Collection; 9tl: Carolyn Shultz ©
Vogue/Condé Nast Publications
Ltd; 9bl: Peter Knapp ©
Vogue/Condé Nast Publications
Ltd; 10bl, 12tl, 14ml/r, 15tl, 18-
19, 21tr, 21br: Alex Chatelain ©
Vogue/Condé Nast Publications
Ltd; 17bc, 24tl: Eric Boman ©
Vogue/Condé Nast Publications
Ltd; 18tl: BBC Picture Archive).

With special thanks to the
Picture Library & Syndication
Department at Vogue
Magazine/Condé Nast
Publications Ltd.

*An explanation of difficult
words can be found in the
glossary on page 30.*

20TH CENTURY fashion

THE 70s

PUNKS, GLAM ROCKERS & NEW ROMANTICS

Sarah Gilmour

Heinemann LIBRARY

CONTENTS

THE GLAM & GLOSSY '70S
5

RETRO DRESSING
6

THE MYSTIC ORIENT
8

GLAM & GLITTER
10

EVERYDAY FASHION
12

PHYSICAL FASHION
14

DISCO BABES & DANCING QUEENS
16

URBAN WARRIORS
18

DENIM FOR EVERYONE
20

PUNK FASHION
22

THE NEW ROMANTICS
24

JAPANESE FASHION
26

THE TECHNOLOGY BEHIND THE FASHIONS OF THE '70S
28

GLOSSARY
30

TIMELINE
30

INDEX
32

The mini was reinvented with shorter-than-short, tight-fitting hotpants.

The GLAM & GLOSSY '70s

Glamorous, frivolous and more-than-slightly ridiculous, for many people platforms and flares now epitomize 'the decade that style forgot'.

However, there was more to the 1970s than extreme fashions. It was a turbulent, often violent decade. The Vietnam conflict remained unresolved and wars raged in the Middle East. The oil crisis contributed to the recession and rising unemployment in the West, while political scandals provoked still greater unrest.

On marches and demos marginalized groups including blacks, women and gays fought for the right to be treated as equals. Protest also took a violent turn. 'Political' groups resorted to guerrilla techniques, such as letter-bombs and hijacks, to get their message across.

Hippie ideals of peace and love were abandoned in favour of personal gain. Health and fitness became a major craze and people looked for ways to escape through the nostalgia or fantasy of film and fashion.

Fashion reflected many of the decade's changes and obsessions. Army surplus and retro styles were both popular. The glamour of disco and chaos of punk were different reactions to the same depressing surroundings. It was a decade characterised by extremes, a more informal approach to dressing and a greater choice of styles for everyone.

Crazes for disco and glam created a fashion for all that glistened.

Wearing a gas mask, a protester joins in a CND demo ('71) against nuclear weapons.

There were political scandals, such as Watergate in the United States. President Nixon made history as the first president to resign from office ('74). Burglars connected with officials in his government had been caught in the opposition party's headquarters.

Outrageous fashions of the '70s included ankle-breaking platform boots.

RETRO *dressing*

In search of romance, some designers harked back to art deco. Soft, feminine colours included moss green and aubergine.

People who had aspired to peace and love in the 1960s were disillusioned. There were still wars, rising unemployment and social inequality. Fashion escaped the present by turning to the past.

DROPPING OUT

Ageing hippies used clothing to express their disgust at the commercial Western world. The fashion industry was a part of this consumer society, so they bought second-hand clothes from junk shops and vintage clothing stalls or made their own. Lace blouses, long skirts and button boots were mixed with ethnic shawls and handmade sweaters.

RETRO ROMANCE

Designers were quick to pick up on hippie styles. Bill Gibb (1943–88) mixed Celtic and historical references. Zandra Rhodes (*b.*1940) based her 1970 collections on the Ukrainian shawl and Native American clothing. Ossie Clark (1942–96) led the revival for high-necked, Edwardian blouses teamed with floor-length skirts. Laura Ashley (1925–85), who opened her first shop in '67, popularized the milkmaid look, with her feminine and delicate, flowery fabrics based on country prints.

A sheer blouse and a silk patchwork skirt created an Eastern ethnic look.

HOLLYWOOD GLAMOUR

Historic influences were also used to create a far darker, more glamorous retro-chic. The fashions of the 1920s, '30s and particularly the '40s were revisited. Second-hand shops were again raided, this time for little dresses in 'trashy' fabrics such as rayon. Teamed with platform shoes and (fake) fur coats, such outfits recreated the image of '40s film stars.

The film Bonnie and Clyde ('67) *starring Fay Dunaway and Warren Beatty, had popularized the '30s style.*

Bold, sporting checks harked back to the country casual look of men in the '20s.

ART DECO

The fashion for 1930s art deco was epitomized by the shop Biba, owned by Barbara Hulanicki (*b.*1936). In '73 Biba moved into an old building with an art deco interior. In 1972 Karl Lagerfeld (*b.*1938) produced a Deco collection for the French ready-to-wear label, Chloé.

RETRO MOVIES

Bonnie and Clyde was as much about attitude as it was about the clothes. Bank robbers on the run, Clyde wore a double-breasted suit, Bonnie a knee-length, A-line skirt and beret (soon to be copied on the catwalks and in the high street). Other films which inspired retro fashions were *The Boyfriend* ('71), in which model Twiggy played a '20s flapper, and *Cabaret* ('72), set in '30s Berlin and starring Liza Minnelli.

Oxford bags, first worn by men in the '20s, had been adopted by women as leisure wear in the '30s. Now they became the alternative to flares.

PERSONAL TASTE

Fashion was no longer something to be slavishly followed as it changed each season. Individuality was far more important. People could avoid the mainstream in favour of styles which set them apart from the crowd and which were often associated with a particular way of life.

The MYSTIC Orient

From the hippies at the opening of the decade to the new romantics at its close, the influence of the East on Western fashion was a recurring theme.

WEST GOES EAST

Why the fascination with the East? During the 1970s the Middle East was rarely out of the headlines. The Yom Kippur War ('73) and the resultant raising of oil prices by 70 per cent caused a global crisis. A craze for all things Egyptian took Britain by storm as over one-and-a-half million people flocked to see the artefacts from Tutankhamun's tomb exhibited at the British Museum ('72). With air travel cheaper than ever, more people were holidaying in exotic locations. And the interest in health helped to popularize exotic exercise such as yoga and t'ai chi.

The stunning turban was an exotic accessory which brought a sense of mystique and romance to western fashion.

PICK & MIX

Of course, eastern influences on fashion were not specifically a phenomenon of the 1970s. However they fitted in with the popular themes of the decade: fantasy, glamour, escapism, nostalgia and the continuing quest for novelty. Designers picked up on elements of traditional costume which interested them, transformed them into fashion garments and then moved on to something new.

ZANDRA RHODES

More than any other designer in the '70s, Zandra Rhodes was influenced by other cultures and countries, from Mexico to Australia. In '79 she visited China and was inspired by the headdresses and strong make-up worn in Chinese opera. She decorated her fabrics with circular designs based on the stone carvings of water and clouds in ancient Chinese palaces. Some of her finished garments reflected Chinese architecture: one blouse had pagoda sleeves. Rhodes also drew heavily on Chinese clothing itself, employing traditional techniques such as quilting.

Rhodes's dramatic creations sell worldwide.

ASIA & THE PACIFIC

Turbans were revived as part of the retro-chic look, while sarongs were adopted as beachwear. Turkish harem pants were popular for eveningwear, as was the kaftan, a loose, ankle-length robe believed to have originated in ancient Mesopotamia. All these items appeared in modern fabrics and cuts to give them a western flavour.

Borrowings from the Orient were recreated in ultra-modern materials. This coolie hat ('77), became a fashion item when made in blue PVC.

GYPSY CHIC

Eastern Europe seemed just as exotic. The gypsy look, characterised by flounced skirts, low necklines and colourful sashes and scarves, was exploited by designers such as Caroline Charles (*b*.1942) and Thea Porter (*b*.1927).

COSSACK COUTURE

Yves Saint Laurent (*b*.1936) turned to Russia for inspiration: in 1976 he sent his models down the cat-walk in baggy trousers tucked into cossack boots, full flowing dresses and fur hats. Decoration included braiding, embroidery and brocade. Pure fairytale, these clothes were far beyond the means of the average woman. Even so, they presented a silhouette that could be copied.

This paddy-field look of '73 by Kenzo was for his own shop, Jungle Jap, opened in '70.

GLAM & GLITTER

Marc Bolan, lead singer of T Rex, exploited his good looks. He wore his hair shoulder-length and his suits glittery.

In a decade of outrageous fashions, glam was the most outrageous by far. The 1940s platforms, padded shoulders, flares and synthetic fabrics were adopted by serious and not-so-serious rock stars and mutated into spectacular stage costumes.

FACTORY-MADE

In the 1960s and '70s pop artist Andy Warhol (1928–87) and followers at his studio, the Factory, were a huge influence on art, film and fashion. Transvestite film star Candy Darling and performance band the Exploding Plastic Inevitable set the tone for sexual ambiguity and dressing up which were to be key elements of glam style.

GLAM ROCKERS

Glam rock spawned a new generation of superstars whose appeal depended as much on their image as their music. Performers such as the New York Dolls, Alice Cooper, T Rex and David Bowie strutted the stage in face paint and feather boas. Platform boots got higher, flares got wider and hair got longer. Satin, velvet and suede were the favourite fabrics – all liberally sprinkled with sequins. Make-up was essential: eyeliner and glitter eyeshadow were worn by the guys as well as the girls.

Calvin Klein's bronze suede jacket and gold gauze trousers ('79) demonstrate truly over-the-top glamour.

High-fashion designers including Kansai Yamamoto borrowed elements of glam, such as these high-rise boots.

THE IMPACT OF GLAM

Such wild attire was not really meant for daily wear – 20-cm-high platform boots made it pretty hard to run for a bus! And you only need to look at the audiences on the music shows such as *Top of the Pops* to see the difference between stage and streetwear. While Alice Cooper sang *School's Out* ('72) wearing leather flares and running mascara, bewildered schoolkids jigged around in frilly apron dresses or tank tops. However, high-street equivalents of glam outfits could be found at shops such as Paraphernalia in New York and Mr Freedom in London.

In the early '70s, hotpants – short shorts in satin or suede – replaced the miniskirt.

CHANGING IDEAS

Without the permissiveness that began in the 1960s, glam would never have existed. While it may look silly today, the posturing of glam rockers made the idea of homosexuality or bisexuality less of a taboo – even though most of these dolled-up musicians were heterosexual.

FANTASY WORLD

Glam fashion delighted in the extreme, the tacky and the shocking. But as it was mainly confined to the stage, in the end it was more about fantasy and escapism than a serious attempt at changing society.

SPACE ODDITY

With his dyed hair, make-up and earrings, David Bowie paraded costumes that included sequined leotards and thigh-high platform boots. He was the most outrageous performer of the decade. His androgynous look shocked the older generation but inspired the young to question traditional roles.

In the '70s David Bowie re-invented himself several times – as Ziggy Stardust and Aladdin Sane.

EVERYDAY *fashion*

Not everyone liked glam and retro fashions. By 1973 the novelty was wearing thin. Mainstream fashion avoided these extreme styles and began catering to the increasing demand for classic, wearable clothing.

A crepe-de-Chine A-line suit ('78) was the perfect office wear.

HARD TIMES

Recession, high unemployment and increasing inflation in the early 1970s meant many people simply couldn't afford to spend as much on fashion. Even those who could did not want to advertise their wealth. For the first time in fashion, dressing down became more important than dressing up.

THE END OF COUTURE?

With the fragmentation of fashion, the number of different styles to choose from and the rise of alternative and anti-fashions, many thought that the 1970s would see the decline of haute couture. But in response to changing attitudes, designers began to focus on the market for classic clothes, producing prêt-à-porter or ready-to-wear collections which were more profitable than haute couture.

THE OIL CRISIS
The Yom Kippur War ('73) led to cuts in oil deliveries to the West. Rising prices and oil shortages resulted in inflation, recession and unemployment. A miner's strike cut off coal supplies to power stations ('74). This crisis was reflected in the sober fashions of the period.

In Britain in '73 a three-day week and lighting restrictions were imposed to try to conserve energy.

Men still wore suits to work, but the silhouette was more informal. Yves Saint Laurent's collection of '74 featured trousers with flared legs.

READY-TO-WEAR

Jean Muir (1933–95), Sonia Rykiel (*b*.1930) and Yves Saint Laurent were key figures in this fashion revolution. Muir and Rykiel were both renowned for their elegant, fluid garments in jersey; masculine tailored suits, known as *smoking*s, were Saint Laurent's trademark. These were adopted by the newly-liberated women who had fought for recognition in the workplace. But American designers, such as Ralph Lauren (*b*.1939) and Calvin Klein (*b*.1942) were best at these relaxed classics.

CAPSULE CHIC

Tweed jackets, knee-length skirts, slim-cut trousers, knitwear and smart blouses became the basics of the working woman's wardrobe. Easily combined into a number of outfits, this idea of a capsule wardrobe has had a lasting effect on how we dress. Another innovation was 'seasonless dressing' which meant women were not forced to change their look every season, but could wear the same pieces over several years, adding co-ordinating items. The emphasis was on cheap chic: *Vogue* introduced its 'More Dash Less Cash' feature.

Stars of the TV hit Charlie's Angels *sported fashionable flicked-back hair and outsize collars.*

HEALTHY GOOD LOOKS

A natural look for hair and make-up complemented the classic outfit. Models such as Lauren Hutton kept make-up to a minimum with soft peaches and pinks. Hair was shoulder-length, shiny and flicked from the face. Good health and a slim figure were achieved by what were to become 1970s obsessions: diet and exercise.

Woody Allen's movie Annie Hall *promoted a look of effectively thrown-together separates.*

PHYSICAL *fashion*

The 1970s saw a new craze for working out. Designers such as Ralph Lauren, Yves Saint Laurent and Calvin Klein were producing figure-hugging fashions that required well-toned bodies.

Working her body, the actress-turned-aerobics-queen Jane Fonda did wonders for the Lycra leotard, leg warmers and, of course, her own exercise videos.

LET'S GET PHYSICAL

To get their bodies in shape, men and women visited the gym, took up jogging, cycling or even marathon running. These activities required specific types of clothing and initially there was little to choose from.

But soon sportswear designers recognised the rapidly expanding market. Tracksuits and running shoes left the gym and hit the streets. New aerobics and dance classes helped popularize leotards and leg warmers.

The aptly-named boob tube was a sexy interpretation of dancewear that left little to the imagination.

DESIGNER SPORTSWEAR

Betsey Johnson (*b*.1942) brought out inspired bodysuits, leotards and hot pants. Basic items, such as a Windbreaker or sweatshirt were given a fashionable twist – designers cut the fabric closer to the body and used fabrics such as terry towelling or velour and contrasting piping.

Stylish designer Joseph created this practical cotton tracksuit featured in Vogue, *summer '79.*

WORK & PLAY

Women wanted to show off the bodies they had worked so hard to achieve. In France, Sonia Rykiel popularized clinging, slinky knitwear; in the United States, body-conscious clothes were a speciality. Many designers were influenced by Claire McCardell (1905–58) who, in the 1940s, had taken simple fabrics such as denim and made 'playwear'.

EASY STYLES

Physical fashion was all about feeling comfortable and appearing relaxed. Men and women needed smart, casual clothes and there was less of a distinction between day and evening wear. Sportswear provided an easy solution, while jazzed-up versions in silks, satins, Lurex or Spandex made perfect disco clobber. Practical or sexy, sportswear offered an alternative to the extremes of fashion and taste that have become the trademark of the 1970s.

GAME, SET & MATCH
The sports craze started with the tennis boom. Players such as Björn Borg and Chris Evert were like pop stars. Slazenger, Head and Adidas re-vamped tennis whites and added items such as matching sweat bands. And it was possible to buy the same style shirt that Borg wore on court.

Chris Evert wore a dress which bridged the gap between sport and fashion.

Dance studios sprang up, selling soft leather ballet pumps, leotards and leg warmers.

DISCO *babes &* DANCING *queens*

Disco favourites The Jackson Five wore glitzy disco outfits as standard stage wear.

Discomania swept the United States and then Europe at the end of the 1970s. At clubs such as Studio 54 in New York, stars like Bianca Jagger, Calvin Klein, Elizabeth Taylor and Andy Warhol were all regulars. Discothèques created a fantasy world where the light shows dazzled, the music thumped and real life was left at the door.

WHAT TO WEAR?

With disco came glamour and a return to dressing up. On the crowded dance floor, eye-catching fashions were necessary to attract attention. Choosing what to wear added to the excitement – and what a choice there was…

DISCO STYLE

Almost anything went but since the main activities at a disco were dancing and posing, freedom to move was crucial and clothes had to look good under the powerful laser lights.

A Vogue model teamed a stretchy Lycra bodysuit with a blue sequined jacket ('78).

16

DISCO DESIGNERS

Many of the people at the most exclusive clubs were in the fashion business. Roy Halston (1932–90) and Stephen Burrows (*b.*1943) were the kings of disco. For those who could afford his prices, Halston produced halter-neck dresses and jumpsuits in jersey, chiffon and Ultrasuede. Burrows was famous for his crinkled, 'lettuce-leaf' hems and patchwork trousers. Most outrageous of all was the futuristic look, with body glitter and sequins, silver and gold lamé, or a Thierry Mugler jumpsuit; but not everyone was so extreme!

ANYTHING GOES

For those on a budget, sportswear was a cheap option and included satin running shorts teamed with skimpy vests. A trashy sequined evening-dress, worn with kitsch accessories, was also acceptable. The American preppie style of jeans, button-down shirt and sneakers, although completely at odds with the disco aesthetic, was often seen on the dance floor, too.

DANCES WITH WHEELS

Roller-disco developed its own brand of fashion. Companies such as Danskin in the United States produced leotards, bodysuits and tights in brightly-coloured Spandex with matching wrap-around skirts. Stretchy Spandex was the practical choice for this pursuit, teamed with knee- and elbow-pads and a crash helmet. Ready to roll!

Roller-disco combined both the craze for disco and for roller-skating.

Pearly green sequins and spike heels: sexy eveningwear for the most glamorous disco babes.

URBAN *warriors*

A period of protest, the 1970s saw a number of minority groups campaigning for equal rights. Anti-war protest also continued until the United States army withdrew from Vietnam in '73.

Power to the people! Dressed in his army surplus, Citizen Smith's Wolfie was the ultimate urban warrior.

Designers exploited classic military tailoring to create outfits for the assertive, independent woman. The severity of a high-necked khaki jacket ('78) was offset by vampish make-up.

MILITARY STYLES

The anti-war protesters dressed in army surplus in a parody of the soldiers they opposed. With cheap combat pants, long hair and a radical attitude, they aimed to undermine all that a uniform stood for. With US troops on the news nightly and the success of *M*A*S*H* (the anti-war black comedy set in Korea), army surplus soon filtered into fashion.

LEATHER-CLAD BOYS

Gay men had by far the most flamboyant approach to fashion. By adopting the most macho of styles and flaunting them openly, they confused the whole idea of masculinity. Not just army surplus, but also workwear was adopted, such as plaid shirts, denim dungarees and, of course, leather.

Gay men wore wild leather concoctions to proudly proclaim their sexuality.

WOMEN'S LIBBERS

In 1971 Germaine Greer's *The Female Eunuch* urged women to free themselves from men and male values. Across the Western world women burned their bras, stopped dressing to please men and no longer shaved their legs. The strict rules of fashion and beauty seemed outdated. The '70s became a decade in which women had to fight for equal pay and which ended with a woman as prime minister in Britain. To do this, women felt they had to abandon traditional ideals of fashion.

Richard Roundtree became a style icon as the supercool star of Shaft *('71), playing a black private eye.*

SERIOUS CLOTHES

Whether these campaigners were fighting the cause of blacks, gays or feminists, each became associated with specific forms of dress and created their own kind of uniform.

BLACK PANTHERS

The Black Panther party formed in '66 to fight for the rights of black Americans and was active throughout the '70s. Black pride was a significant force in the '70s: the afro hairstyle in particular symbolized black culture.

Black leather jackets and black berets became the revolutionary fashion statement for many people.

Russian military styling gave an air of icy, moody chic.

People could clearly show what views they held by the clothes they wore. By selecting clothes which were obviously not fashionable – and therefore not subject to constant change – people were able to indicate the serious and permanent nature of their cause. Clothes had become a form of silent communication. Of course, anti-fashion soon became a fashion in its own right.

DENIM *for everyone*

In the 1850s Levi Strauss began making tough work trousers from a fabric called denim. Originally they were for use by American goldminers but by World War II jeans had become indispensable workwear. The 1950s saw the newly-named teenagers adopt jeans as their own, and in the '60s, jeans were mutated into frayed and embroidered flares. By the '70s, denim had begun to appeal to just about everyone.

THE FIRST JEANS

Denim originated in the French town of Nîmes, hence its name, from the French *serge de Nîmes*. Tailor Levi Strauss had first used canvas to make hard-wearing trousers, but then he came up with the idea of dyed denim instead. It was a hit! By 1873, he had patented a version of his trousers that used copper rivets to provide extra strength.

Californian gold prospectors in the 1850s were the first to wear denim Levi's.

JEANS FOR ALL

In a decade where there were more fashions to choose from than ever, jeans became a uniform. And there were so many styles of jeans that they could be worn as a part of any look.

FASHION STATEMENT

While for some jeans were ultra-fashionable, others chose them because of their timeless appeal. They were a way to avoid the frivolity of fashion. By the early 1970s, the feminist in jeans or dungarees and the peace protester in frayed flares were stereotypes.

For day-to-day wear, turned-up jeans were worn with a tight-fitting jumper. Patterned, colourful knits were popular.

CUSTOMIZED JEANS

People customized their denims to suit their own style. Hippies embroidered and patched their jeans and in 1973 Levi's recognized the popularity of this by holding a Denim Art Contest. Glam rockers stitched jeans with sequins; punks ripped, pinned and slashed them. Disco girls wore theirs skin-tight with strappy, high-heels and fluorescent socks. Whatever the look, jeans fitted.

Denim was not restricted to jeans. Denim waistcoats and short denim jackets were numerous. Full-length denim coats could be seen too.

A sea of denim: denim was the perfect uniform for pop fans around the world, and still is today.

Denim or no denim, Wild West boots and cowboy hats were popular.

JEANS FOR GROWN-UPS

Denim gained a new respectability which reflected the increasing importance of casual, informal dress. Men and women combined Levi's with button-down shirts, sweaters and loafers for a relaxed, unisex look. Jeans had become a classic.

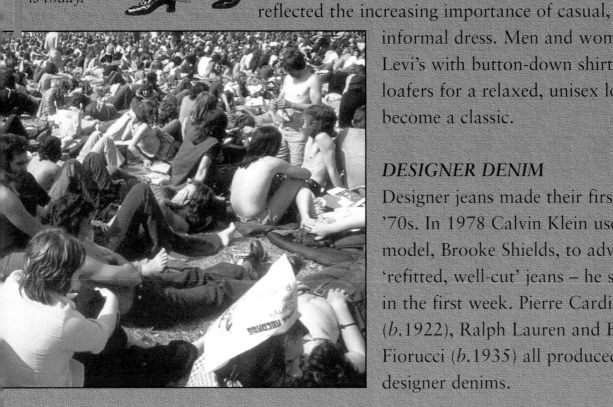

DESIGNER DENIM

Designer jeans made their first appearance in the '70s. In 1978 Calvin Klein used a 15-year-old model, Brooke Shields, to advertise his range of 'refitted, well-cut' jeans – he sold 200,000 pairs in the first week. Pierre Cardin (*b*.1922), Ralph Lauren and Elio Fiorucci (*b*.1935) all produced designer denims.

DENIM ... EVERYWHERE!

And it wasn't just jeans that came in denim. Everything that could be made up in denim was, from the traditional work shirt to hats, bags, bikinis and shoes. Your car seats could be covered in denim. You could dream beneath a denim duvet – or even buy a denim radio!

Dungarees, worn comfortably here with lace-up boots, provided practical, although not always flattering, fashion for both men and women.

PUNK *fashion*

Punk was born in Malcolm McLaren and Vivienne Westwood's shop, Sex, in 1975. McLaren asked a regular visitor to the shop, John Lydon, if he would join a band he was managing called the Sex Pistols. Soon the band was making headlines with their bad behaviour: spitting and vomiting on stage and swearing in public.

Aggressive do-it-yourself piercing, as demonstrated by this Swedish girl, was soon the punk stereotype.

FETISH WEAR

Westwood and McLaren opened the shop, first called Let it Rock, on London's Kings Road in 1972. They sold copies of teddy-boy drape suits, the uniform of young rebels in the '50s. By '75, the shop was selling the black rubber and leather fetish wear that gave it its name, and was a mecca for young punks.

NO FUTURE

Britain in the mid-1970s was a depressing place for a teenager. With high unemployment, kids felt they had no hope and no future. Even music felt stale and pointless: teeny boppers like Donny Osmond or dressed-up glam rockers had nothing to say about real life.

Punk hair was dyed in dayglo colours: yellow, green, blue, orange or red. Many wore their hair Mohican-style, stiffening it into place with liberal helpings of glue.

The Pistols could not play and they could not sing – but they looked good! McLaren later claimed that he formed the group only to sell more trousers.

The black leather jacket had been a symbol of youth rebellion since the '40s. Punks made it their own by adding chains, studs, badges, safety pins and paint.

BORN IN THE USA

Aggressive and shocking, punk music and fashion captured the anger and frustration felt by many teenagers. Punk styles also flourished in the United States. More subtle than its British equivalent, American punk was never as popular but its influence was crucial. McLaren visited New York in 1973 where he met the New York Dolls and was impressed by the reactions to their outrageous glam outfits.

DIY FASHION

Punks used anti-fashion to express disgust at the aspirations of the middle classes. They adopted items of clothing that were deliberately shocking – and often physically repellent. Pushing safety pins through cheeks, ears and every available area of clothing, they assaulted all notions of taste. Bondage, leather, pornographic prints and swastikas were flaunted in the streets. Suits and school uniforms were ripped, pinned and worn with aggressive make-up and hair, in a parody of respectability. It was a do-it-yourself look and it spelt rebellion.

PUNK CHIC

However shocking, within a very short time punk was seen as an influence on mainstream fashion. By '76 Italian *Vogue* was featuring pages of black clothing worn with aggressive accessories. In '77 Zandra Rhodes unveiled her Punk Chic collection. Punk met haute couture with interesting results: the safety pins and embroidery were gold!

Zandra Rhodes created designer Punk wear.

The <u>New</u> Romantics

Considered a style phenomenon of the early 1980s when it was popularized by bands such as Adam and the Ants and Duran Duran, new romanticism had actually been around since the mid-'70s. However, the media did not invent the term until the beginning of the next decade.

High-heeled boots, feathered hat, ruffled shirt, satin trousers ... but the key to the look was the careful pose!

EARLY DAYS

The early new romantics had punk roots. But they took more interest in their clothes, posing and clubbing than in anarchy, spitting or sweaty pogoing. When punk hit the headlines and chaos reigned, this group of posers went into hiding.

THE NEW ROMANTIC SOUND

Initially the new romantics listened to music by Bowie, Roxy Music and Kraftwerk. This futuristic sound seemed the perfect antidote to bubbly disco pop. But before long, the new romantics were creating pop music for themselves.

Steve Strange and Visage, Boy George and Culture Club and Adam and the Ants cared more for visual effects than for music. Videos began to be used to promote pop music and were an opportunity to flaunt the look.

Theatrical make-up and over-the-top costumes helped Steve Strange to the top of the charts.

In 1978, when punk was dying, these posers re-emerged at 'Bowie Night' in a London nightclub called Gossips. Held on a Tuesday, the club successfully excluded unfashionable weekend clubbers.

WAY-OUT COSTUMES

Art students, Bowie fans and dandies indulged in the retro-dressing and futurism which had already marked other 1970s styles – but went further. Their style was theatrical, exotic or historical. The most extreme went to theatrical costumiers to transform themselves into pirates, space captains or oriental princesses.

Fashion house Chloé's interpretation of the look ('77) featured the essential lace shirt and a cavalier hat with a red ostrich feather.

WHAT'S IN A NAME?

The 'romance' was in frilled shirts, bows, floppy haircuts and velvet knickerbockers. The 'new', futuristic element combined Bowie's Ziggy Stardust era with the military styling of Roxy Music's ultra-cool frontman, Bryan Ferry. New wave bands such as Joy Division and Kraftwerk gave the look a harder edge. They dressed in anonymous suits with skinny ties, or in boilersuits. Malcolm McLaren's shop PX opened in 1978 and initially catered to this industrial look, before transforming into a new romantic boutique. By the turn of the decade, new romantics had moved from the underground to the headlines.

Formed in '77, Adam and the Ants had a shaky start, until singer Adam Ant hired Malcolm McLaren as style guru. McLaren dressed the band in pirate outfits; future looks would include the 'dandy highwayman' and the fairytale 'Prince Charming' ('81).

Hats made a comeback with new romantic clubbers, whether in the form of a military beret or a '40s-inspired jaunty pill-box.

JAPANESE *fashion*

One of the most unexpected influences of the decade came from Japan. The generation of Japanese designers that emerged in the 1970s are now amongst the most respected leaders of the fashion world. As well as being sold in shops across the globe, their radical and intellectual work has been exhibited in art galleries and museums.

Kansai Yamamoto created dramatic, if sometimes impractical, garments from Japanese inspiration ('71).

Kenzo's cropped kimono top and sarong-style skirt ('76) show his trademark bold prints.

KIMONOS & OBIS

The first Japanese to make a name in western fashion was Hanae Mori (*b.*1926). She worked within western traditions but also based many of her designs on the traditional Japanese kimono, a loose, wide-sleeved robe fastened at the waist with a broad sash called an obi.

THE JUNGLE JAP

Kyoto-born Kenzo (*b.*1940) sparked real interest in Japanese fashion when he opened his shop, Jungle Jap, in Paris in 1970.

Although he was not as radical as those who followed, he did make a break from fussy Paris couture. His clothes, often inspired by the bold designs of kabuki theatre, were fun and demonstrated his impressive ability in layering patterns and prints.

SWATHES & LAYERS

In his publication *East Meets West*, Issey Miyake (*b*.1935) explained that western clothes are shaped with the body as the starting point, whereas the Japanese approach is completely different – they start with the fabric, so the emphasis is on layers, textures and patterns. In a decade which favoured figure-hugging clothes, the most radical Japanese fashions appeared utterly unwearable to western eyes.

THE RADICAL GENERATION

Soon Japanese designers were executing their ideas in undiluted form. Issey Miyake combined eastern materials and colour sense with state-of-the-art manufacturing techniques. For his first collection in 1970 he showed jeans in quilted sashiko, a material traditionally used for judo and kendo (fencing) clothes. Kansai Yamamoto (*b*.1944) also used sashiko. He opened his own house in '71 and had his own unique and abstract style, which was heavily influenced by kabuki puppet theatre. Tokyo-born Rei Kawakubo (*b*.1942) had formed fashion company Comme des Garçons in '69. Like Yohji Yamamoto (*b*.1943), she created voluminous garments that disregarded body shape and experimented with torn or tattered fabrics. All of these designers went on to be highly influential in the '80s as, slowly, they revolutionized western attitudes to fashion.

Kansai Yamamoto used a jockey theme of numbers and jodhpurs – with a padded satin kimono!

When unzipped, this dramatic cape, by Yamamoto, revealed a skin-tight playsuit with a matching kabuki mask design.

The TECHNOLOGY *behind*

The most popular fabrics of the 1970s reflect the number of contrasting styles of the time. From the old to the new, the natural to the synthetic, almost every fabric and technique found favour for its own specific qualities.

Retro glamour without cruelty: fake fur made of acrylic and nylon gave an injection of '70s kitsch to the '40s film-star look.

BACK TO BASICS

Not all designers sought hi-tech methods. The love affair with retro extended to the way designers worked. Bill Gibb was renowned for his appliqué eveningwear, on to which ornamental pieces of fabric were sewn or glued. Zandra Rhodes explored every traditional means of producing and decorating fabric. Her designs were hand-printed and her signature garments quilted, embroidered and hand-sewn.

NATURAL FABRICS

Popular fabrics included denim and cheesecloth. Denim, a cotton twill of white and blue threads, was mass-manufactured. It was treated to give a variety of effects, for example by stonewashing, where the fabric was washed with pumice stones to create a soft, faded look. Most cheesecloth was imported from India, where it was embroidered and dyed by hand.

BUILT TO STRETCH

New technological developments in textile production were important for sports-, day- and eveningwear. Lycra, with its unique ability to stretch, keep its shape and improve the drape of a garment, was to change the face of fashion.

Zandra Rhodes in a tunic of her own design. Her textiles were inspired by everything from feathers to cacti and were all made painstakingly by hand.

Model Twiggy was a fan of Bill Gibb's romantically trimmed evening-dresses.

the fashions of the '70s

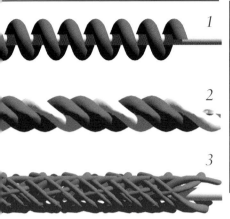

1

2

3

There are different ways to add Lycra to a fibre (above). It can be covered by the fibre (1); it can be twisted with another yarn as it is spun (2); or it can be forced through an air jet with the other fibre, which coats it in a lacework of strands (3).

Lycra is always mixed with another fibre. This gives the resulting fabric maximum stretch and strength and improves its feel and drape, or the way it hangs. Right, strands of Lycra (white) are interwoven with cotton jersey (purple) to create super-stretchy sportswear.

Introduced by the company Du Pont in 1958, Lycra was a trademarked type of Spandex. By the '70s Lycra was being used for swimwear and leotards as well as underwear. Because it clung to the body, dried within minutes and always kept its shape, it made a practical fabric not only for sports- and dancewear, but also for disco fashions.

SLINKY SYNTHETICS

Synthetic or man-made fibres came into their own. Retro-chic revisited fabrics of earlier decades such as nylon, rayon, lamé and Lurex. Glam and disco fashions exploited their tacky, slinky properties. Lurex was a metallic thread that spangled as it caught the light and was effective for eveningwear. Rayon had been invented as a synthetic alternative to silk and, in the '70s, was flower-printed to make '40s-style frocks. What the people who designed and wore '70s clothes proved more than anything, was that the more fabrics and technologies available, the more wild and inventive fashion becomes.

Lycra's stretchiness made it a perfect fabric for sportswear.

Lamé is a fabric containing metallic threads that glitter and shine. Clever weaving can create patterns, such as these intricate gold flowers ('76).

GLOSSARY

ARMY SURPLUS Ex-military clothes and equipment which are sold at low prices.

ART DECO A decoration and art style based on geometric shapes and strong colours. Art deco originated during the mid-1920s.

BLACK PANTHER PARTY A militant black political party which was active in the USA in the 1960s and 1970s.

BODYSUIT A close-fitting, swimsuit-like garment, which sometimes incorporates footless leggings.

CAPSULE WARDROBE A small collection of co-ordinates that are interchangeable.

DUNGAREES Loose trousers with a bib and shoulder straps attached.

FLARES Trousers that fit tightly to the thigh, but flare out widely from the knee. Also known as bell-bottoms.

JUMPSUIT A one-piece garment that combines trousers and a long-sleeved top.

KABUKI THEATRE An old type of Japanese theatre, with plays that last from dawn until dusk.

LEG WARMERS Long, woollen, footless socks.

LUREX A shiny, metallic fibre that is woven or knitted with another fibre, such as rayon.

OIL CRISIS A fuel shortage that followed the 1973 decision by OPEC (Organization of Petroleum Exporting Countries) to quadruple the price of oil and restrict production. It resulted in petrol rationing and an economic crisis in the West.

OXFORD BAGS Baggy, cuffed trousers.

PLATFORM SOLE An extra-thick shoe or boot sole.

RECESSION A time of economic difficulty; usually involving business failures and a rise in unemployment.

SARONG A length of fabric, wrapped around the body and tied at the waist or chest.

TANK TOP A short, sleeveless knitted or crocheted top.

ULTRASUEDE A washable, synthetic suede-like fabric.

VELOUR A fabric with a velvet-like pile.

- *The word 'hotpants' coined by* Women's Wear Daily •*Jungle Jap opens in Paris* 1

- *French couturier Coco Chanel dies* •*Kansai Yamamoto opens his fashion house* 1

- *Bill Gibb opens his fashion house* •*Lagerfeld produces his 'Deco' collection* 1

- *Issey Miyake has his first show in Paris* •*Levi's hold their Denim Art Contest* 1

- *Jeff Banks launches Warehouse* 1

- *Punk style is born as McLaren & Westwood open their Kings Road shop, Sex* 1

- *Vivienne Westwood's 'Bondage' collection* •*St Laurent's 'Russian' collection* 1

- *Zandra Rhodes: 'Punk Chic' collection* •*Jean-Paul Gaultier starts his company* 1

- *Brooke Shields models Calvin Klein's new 'designer jeans'* 1

- *Death of Norman Hartnell, dressmaker to Queen Elizabeth II* 1

TIMELINE

WORLD EVENTS	TECHNOLOGY	FAMOUS PEOPLE	ART & MEDIA
70 •US troops sent into Cambodia •Chile: Allende elected president	•First video cassette recorders launched on market	•The Beatles split up	•Germaine Greer: The Female Eunuch •Andrew Lloyd Webber: Jesus Christ Superstar
71 •Uganda: Idi Amin seizes power •Indo-Pakistan war results in independent Bangladesh	•USSR launches first space station, Salyut 1 •OMNIMAX cinema invented	•Muhammad Ali loses world heavyweight title to Joe Frazier	•David Bowie: Starman •Ken Russell: The Devils•Stanley Kubrick: Clockwork Orange
72 •SALT I treaty signed by US & USSR •Britain imposes direct rule in Ulster	•First video games devised •First electronic calculator developed	•Bobby Fischer takes world chess title from Boris Spassky	•Tutankhamun exhibition in London •F. Ford Coppola: The Godfather
73 •Yom Kippur War •OPEC oil price increases lead to economic crisis in West	•Skylab space station launched by USA •Mountain bike invented	•Salvador Allende assassinated	•Jørn Utzon's Sydney Opera House is completed
74 •Turkey invades & occupies one-third of Cyprus	•First practical wave-powered generator devised	•US President Nixon resigns over Watergate •Harold Wilson is British prime minister	•Fellini: Amarcord •ABBA: Waterloo
75 •End of Vietnam War •Cambodia overrun by Pol Pot's Khmer Rouge	•French company, BIC, invent the disposable razor •First ultralight tested	•Spanish fascist dictator Franco dies; King Juan Carlos restored to throne	•Steven Spielberg: Jaws •Queen: Bohemian Rhapsody
76 •S. Africa: Soweto riots result in more than 200 deaths	•US Viking probes drop landers on Mars •First commercial flight of Concorde	•Death of Mao	•Christo: Running Fence environmental sculpture •Bob Marley: Rastaman Vibration
77 •UN bans arms sales to S. Africa	•Apple II personal computer launched by Jobs & Wozniak •Speed sailing invented	•Steve Biko dies in S. African police custody •Death of Elvis Presley	•Derek Jarman: Jubilee •Sex Pistols: God Save the Queen •Pompidou Centre, Paris, completed
78 •Camp David peace treaty signed by Egypt & Israel		•Louise Brown, first test-tube baby, born •Death of Golda Meir	•John Travolta stars in Saturday Night Fever
79 •Iran: Khomeini comes to power •Uganda: Amin deposed	•Sony Walkman invented •Erno Rubic devised his cube puzzle	•Thatcher becomes Britain's first woman prime minister	•Frank Stella: Kastura •Woody Allen: Manhattan

INDEX

Adam Ant 24, 25
Alice Cooper 10, 11
anti-fashion 12, 19, 23
army surplus clothing 18, 30
art deco 6, 7, 30
Ashley, Laura 6

beret 7, 19
Biba 7
Black Panthers 19, 30
bodysuit 15, 16, 17, 30
Bonnie and Clyde 7
boot 5, 6, 9, 11, 21, 24
Bowie, David 10, 11, 24, 25
Boy George 24
Burrows, Stephen 17

capsule wardrobe 13, 30
Cardin, Pierre 21
Charles, Caroline 9
cheesecloth 28
chiffon 17
Chloé 7, 25
Clark, Ossie 6
classic style 12–13
Comme des Garçons 27

dance, *see* disco style
Danskin 17
denim 15, 18, 20–21, 28
designer jeans 21
discomania 16
disco style 5, 15, 16–17, 21, 29
dress 9, 17
dungarees 18, 20, 21, 30
Du Pont 29

embroidery 9, 20, 21, 28

fabric 7, 9, 10, 15, 17, 20, 27, 28–29
fake fur 7, 28
Female Eunuch, The 19
Fiorucci, Elio 21

flares 5, 10, 11, 20, 21, 30
Fonda, Jane 14

gay style 18
Gibb, Bill 6, 28
glam style 5, 10–11, 21, 23, 29
gypsy look 9

hairstyle 13, 18, 22, 25
Halston, Roy 17
hat 9, 21, 24, 25
haute couture 12, 23
hippie 5, 6, 8, 21
hotpants 4, 11, 15
Hulanicki, Barbara 7

jacket 13, 18, 19, 21, 23
Japanese designers 26–27
jeans 17, 20–21, 27
jersey (fabric) 13, 17, 29
Johnson, Betsey 15
jumpsuit 17, 30
Jungle Jap 27

kabuki theatre 27, 30
kaftan 9
Kawakubo, Rei 27
Kenzo 26, 27
kimono 26, 27
Klein, Calvin 10, 13, 14, 16, 21
knitwear 13, 15, 20
Kraftwerk 24, 25

lace 6, 25
Lagerfeld, Karl 7
lamé 9, 17, 29
Lauren, Ralph 13, 14, 21
leather 11, 18, 19, 22, 23
leg warmer 14, 15, 30
leotard 11, 14, 15, 17, 29
Levi's, *see* jeans
Lurex 15, 29, 30
Lycra 14, 28–29

make-up 10, 13, 18, 24

McCardell, Claire 15
McLaren, Malcolm 22, 23, 25
Miyake, Issey 27
Mohican hairstyle 22
Mori, Hanae 26
Mr Freedom 11
Mugler, Thierry 17
Muir, Jean 13

new romantic style 8, 24–25
New York Dolls 10, 23
nylon 28, 29

oil crisis 5, 8, 12, 30
oriental style 8–9
Oxford bags 7, 30

Paraphernalia 11
platform sole 5, 7, 10, 11, 27, 30
Porter, Thea 9
preppie style 17
prêt-à-porter, *see* ready-to-wear clothing
protest, political 5, 18
punk style 5, 21, 22–23, 24, 25

rayon 7, 29
ready-to-wear clothing 12–13
recession 5, 12, 30
retro style 5, 6–7, 9, 25, 28, 29
Rhodes, Zandra 6, 8, 23, 28
roller-disco 17
Roxy Music 24, 25
rubber 22
Rykiel, Sonia 13, 15

Saint Laurent, Yves 9, 12, 13, 14
sarong 9, 30
satin 10, 15, 17, 24, 27
Saturday Night Fever 17

second-hand clothing 6, 7
sequins 10, 11, 17, 21
Sex (clothes shop) 22
Sex Pistols 22
shoe 17, 21
  see also boot
silk 15
skirt 6, 7, 9, 13, 17
Spandex 15, 17, 29
sportswear 14–15, 17, 29
Strange, Steve 24
Strauss, Levi 20
suede 10, 11
suit 7, 12, 13, 25
sweater 6, 21
sweatshirt 15

tank top 11, 30
terry towelling 15
tracksuit 14, 15
Travolta, John 17
trousers 9, 10, 12, 13, 17, 20, 24
turban 8, 9
Tutankhamun exhibition 8
Twiggy 7, 28

Ultrasuede 17, 30
unemployment 5, 6, 12, 22

velour 15, 30
velvet 10, 25
Vietnam War 5, 18
vintage clothing 6
Vogue magazine 13, 15, 23

Warhol, Andy 10, 16
Westwood, Vivienne 22
workwear 18, 20

Yamamoto, Kansai 11, 26, 27
Yamamoto, Yohji 27
yarn 29
Yom Kippur War 8, 12